UCD WOMEN'S CENTER

The
Mother Daughter
Dance

THE MOTHER DAUGHTER DANCE

WRITTEN AND ILLUSTRATED BY

Jeannie Cochran DuBose

LONGSTREET PRESS

Atlanta, Georgia

LONGSTREET
PRESS

Published by
LONGSTREET PRESS, INC.
2974 Hardman Court
Atlanta, Georgia 30305
www.longstreetpress.net

1st printing, 2004

ISBN: 1-56352-728-6

Printed in the United States of America

Jacket and book design by Burtch Hunter Design LLC

For my mother
and her mother
and her mother . . .

Acknowledgements

There are many godparents to this book. Wonderful, inspiring, talented godparents. Each has nurtured the process, providing their individual imprint of encouragement and criticism. Love and thanks to each of you for continuing to help me believe that this endeavor was more than an elaborate art project on my dining room table. I remain grateful for your support: Lee Billings, Carolyn Brown, Sidney Childress, LaLa Cochran, Catherine Davis, Melissa Devereaux, Bruni Finerty, Amy Grant, Susan Gray, Catherine Meynardi, Shari Moore, Paul Pendergrass, Leslie Pucker, Debbie Schnieder, Sara Sommers, Cynthia Smith, and Barbara Thompson.

Thanks to my father and his enormous personality, who always thinks each one of his children can do anything they put their mind to. Respect for my brother and sister, who have listened to my story many times and have been champs about it. Incredulous wonder for our children, Kirby and John, who didn't disrupt the elaborate art project on the dining room table. Deepest gratitude for my husband and ballast, Richard, whose wry humor and grounded love are invaluable to me. Particular tender acknowledgement for our third child, William Manning DuBose, who was born after this book was written.

THE MOTHER DAUGHTER DANCE IS EVERY WOMAN'S STORY, DRAWN FROM THE RICH MEMORIES OF AN OLDEST DAUGHTER, ARTFULLY TOLD WITH AN ECONOMY OF WORDS AND SOULFUL, PRIMITIVE ILLUSTRATIONS. JEANNIE DUBOSE HAS CAPTURED THIS CIRCLE DANCE WITH A VOICE THAT ECHOES DEEP IN THE BONES. IN THE SEEMINGLY TRIVIAL RITUALS AND ROUTINES OF LIFE, WE POUR OURSELVES INTO EACH OTHER. I HAVE LOVED WATCHING JEANNIE POUR AND PULL BACK AND POUR AGAIN OVER THE YEARS. WE'VE BEEN FRIENDS SINCE CHILDHOOD. AND SO, I CANNOT SEPARATE MYSELF FROM THESE MEMORIES OF PARSLEY AND MUSIC AND CLOSENESS AND DISTANCE . . . AND ALL OF IT CONTINUES TO BE PART OF THE DANCE.

AMY GRANT

JEANNIE DUBOSE'S MOTHER DAUGHTER DANCE IS THE SMARTEST, TRUEST, AND MOST MOVING INVESTIGATION I'VE EVER EXPERIENCED INTO THE MYSTERY OF THIS MOST COMPLEX RELATIONSHIP. HERE'S A BOOK TO READ AGAIN AND AGAIN—A BOOK TO TREASURE. THE BRIGHT AND LOVELY ILLUSTRATIONS SPEAK VOLUMES, SO THIS LITTLE BOOK EXPANDS TO THE SIZE OF A NOVEL IN OUR MINDS. IT'S ILLUMINATING, WISE—AND BEAUTIFUL. A FEAST FOR THE EYES AND HEART ALIKE.

LEE SMITH
AUTHOR, *The Last Girls*

WHETHER YOU HAVE DANCED THE MOTHER DAUGHTER DANCE YOURSELF OR HAVE ONLY WATCHED THOSE YOU LOVE FLINGING EACH OTHER AROUND ON THE DANCE FLOOR, TAKE HEART. THIS GRACEFUL BOOK'S GOOD NEWS IS THAT TIME PASSES AND PARTNERS CHANGE PLACES, GIVING EACH THE CHANCE TO RECOGNIZE HERSELF IN THE OTHER BEFORE THE NEXT GENERATION ARRIVES AND THE DANCE MOVES ON.

BARBARA BROWN TAYLOR
PROFESSOR OF RELIGION, PIEDMONT COLLEGE

Author's Note

It became important to me while in my mid-20s to acknowledge the many dimensions of my relationship with my mother. It was at this point that I found myself trolling through art stores, selecting a variety of papers of different color, texture, and design. Once home with my new supplies, I spent hours and hours cutting and pasting memories of life with my mother. This process was cathartic and powerful for me. I decided to bind these illustrated memories in a book and give them to my mother. With her characteristic grace, she accepted the book and didn't quibble with me over details, perspective, or context.

Fast forward 13 years. Now married, almost 40, and the mother of two, I stumble across the book for the first time since giving it to my mother. I was amazed at my shift in perspective. The story still rang true, but years of motherhood had altered my point of view. Following my husband's advice to "just stay with the process," I spent the next year writing and illustrating a revised book of memories, and began to wonder if the themes in my own story might resonate for other women as well.

As anyone who knows her can attest, my mother, Anita Kirby Cochran, is an amazing woman. Her blessings on my life are beyond measure; her support and encouragement for this book is only the latest expression of a lifetime of love. The Mother Daughter Dance is a tribute to her, and to motherhood, in all of its abundantly human dimensions.

The
Mother Daughter
Dance

I began inside the womb
of a young woman.

Then, and for
nine months after,
she gave me form
and existence.

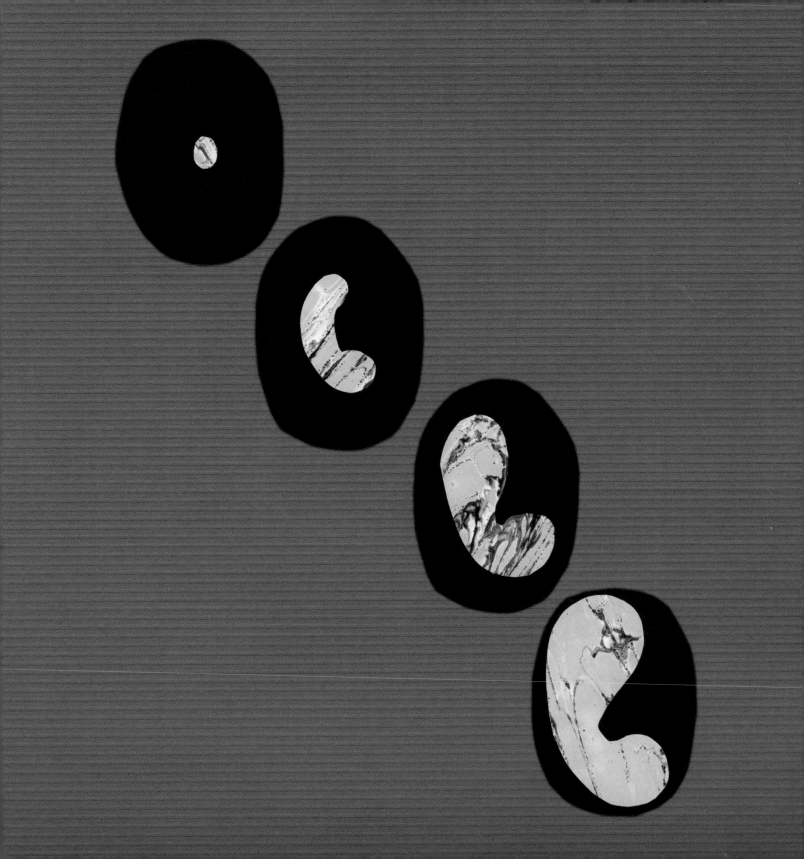

I was born

from her

womb

and into

her arms.

One morning I climbed down from her arms. In the day light, I ran down the sidewalk all by myself. At night I asked my mother to hold me close.

"It's great to be a girl," my mother said. "Girls can wear skirts and pants. They go to school and play sports. They make music. Girls are extra lucky because they can have babies."

When I was three my little sister was born. She was tiny and loud. Before long she was bigger and lots more fun.

My mother drove us to the swimming pool.
She sat in a lounge chair by the pool
with the other mothers.

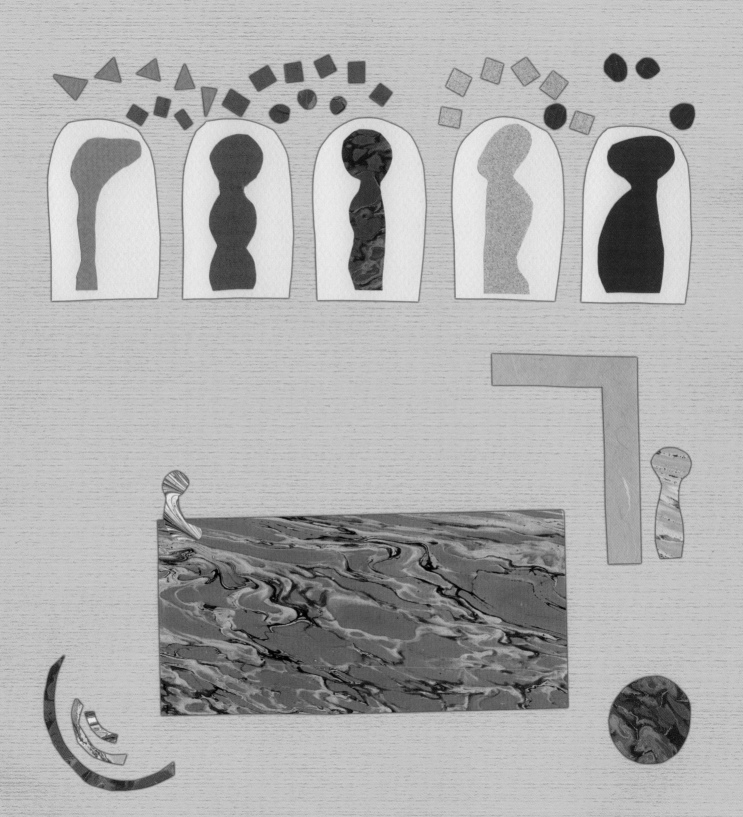

I climbed to the top of the diving board.
"Watch me jump, Mom!" I yelled.
She looked up. When I climbed out
of the water, she said, "Good jump!"

One winter night, when I was
five, it snowed. I was so cold,
I couldn't sleep. My mother piled
blankets on my bed to keep
me warm.

When I learned to draw, I colored a pretty blue face on my mother's book. She was really mad. She crossed her arms tight. Her voice was loud and hard.

That night she came into my room. "I was angry today and said you were a bad girl. You are not a bad girl. Mommy was mad at herself and blamed you." Her voice grew very soft. "You are a good girl."

My mother bought me a pink culotte to wear on my first day of school. At breakfast she said, "This is a big day. I bet you make lots of new friends."

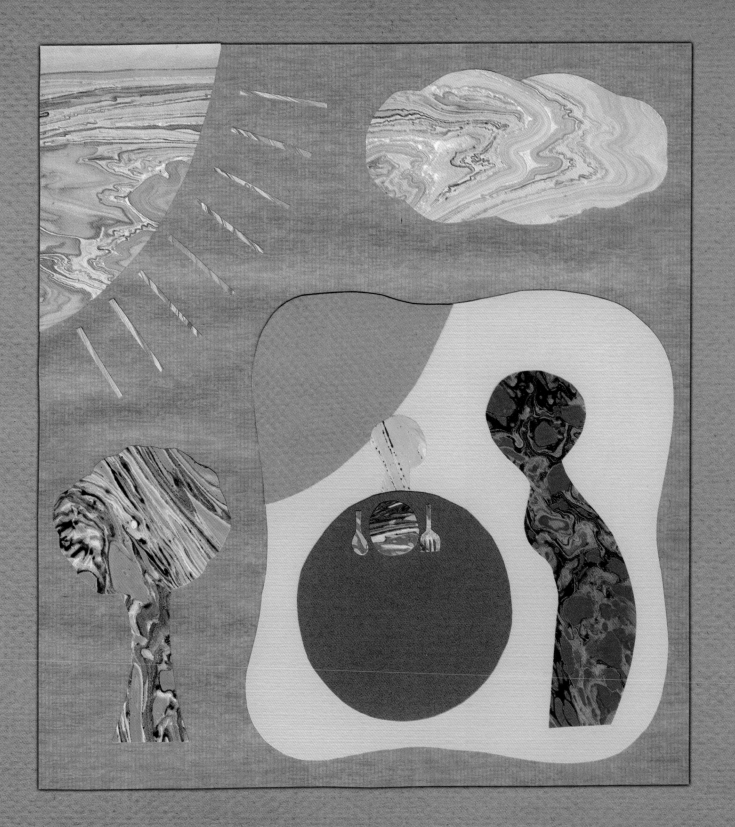

School was a big playground. When I came home, my mother played records and we danced together. "You keep the beat," she said. "You have rhythm like the dancers on T.V."

When I was six my mother's tummy became big like a balloon. "Your brother is inside," she said. I was amazed.

Now we were three. My mother drove us all over town. She drove us to piano. Violin. Basketball. Track. Choir. Wrestling. Scouts. "I spend my whole life in the car," she said.

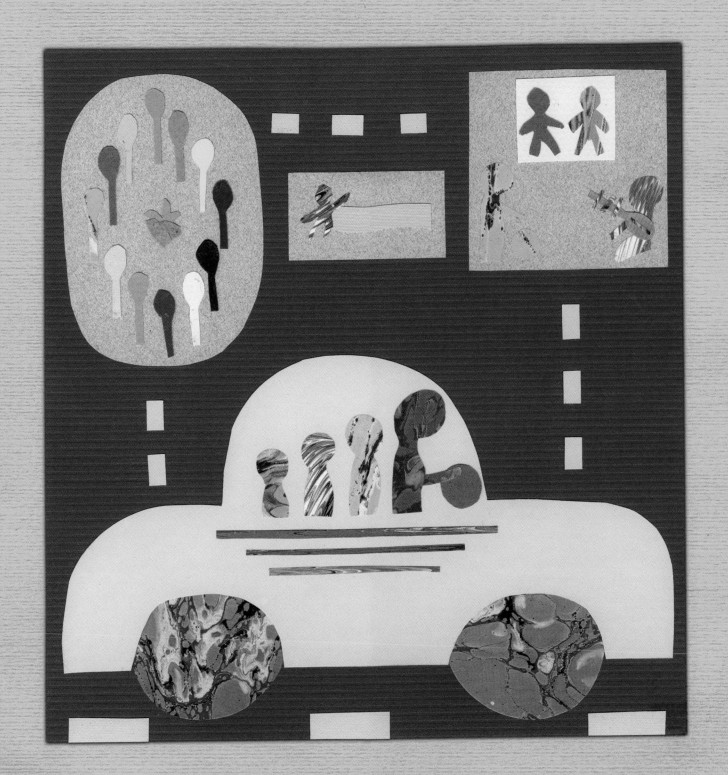

This was not true. My mother was in the kitchen too. Every night she fixed dinner. Sometimes she put parsley on the plate. "For a touch of color," she said. She used a pretty ladle for soups. Sometimes my father came home late for dinner. This made her quiet and mad.

In junior high, I liked my friends better than my family. Some days my mother wore an angry face. Her father, my own PawPaw, was very sick.

Even if we were in the same room, my mother seemed far away. One day in the laundry room my father hugged my mother for a long time. She cried and cried. PawPaw was dying.

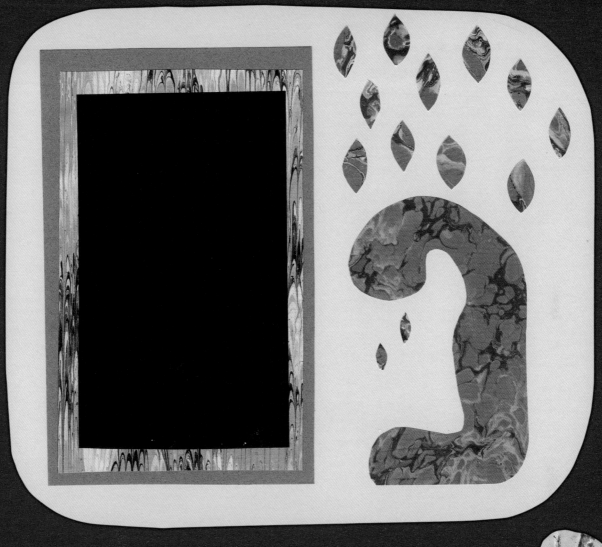
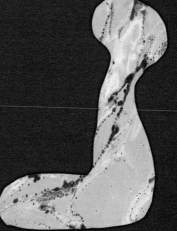

Every year the space between my mother and me grew bigger and bigger. We didn't talk anymore. But my mother and aunt talked all the time. They talked about their mother, my MawMaw.

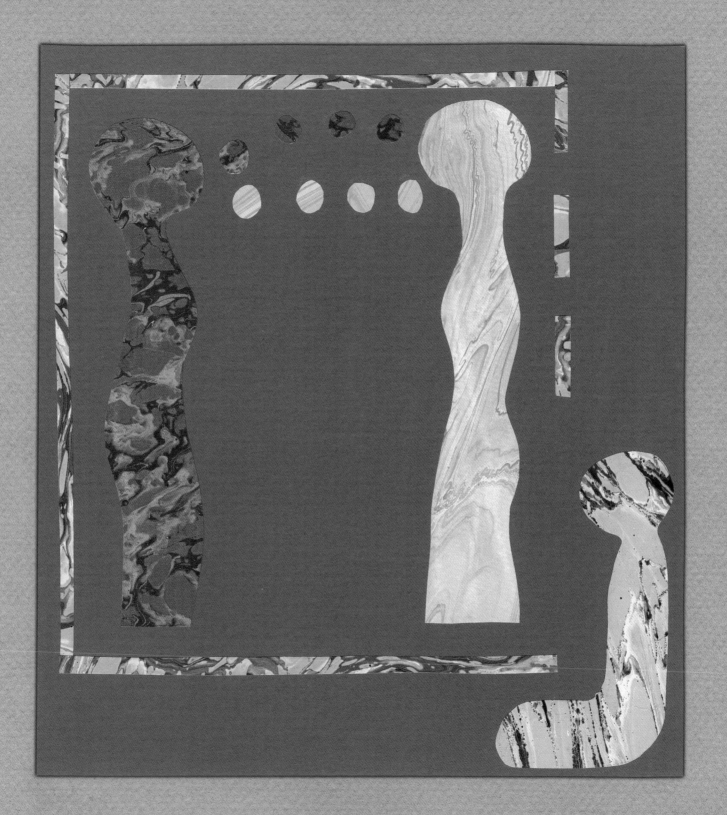

My mother and I lived in the same house but we barely met. My mother could be aloof, distant, even cold. I could be surly, snide, even spiteful.
Things got downright ugly.

One time my mother's words
were so shrill, I felt as though
I'd had the wind
        knocked out of me.

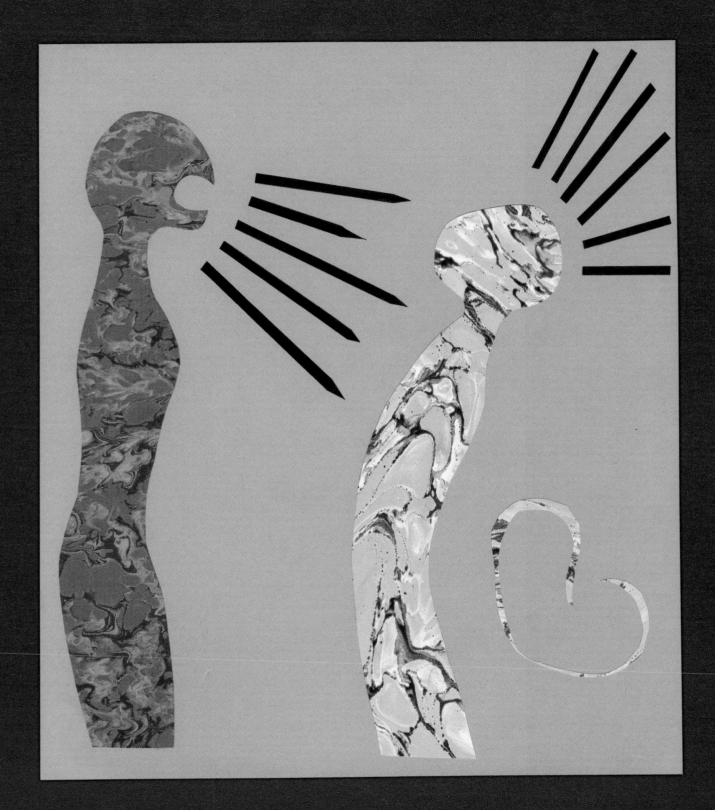

 I tried to knock the wind
right back out of her.

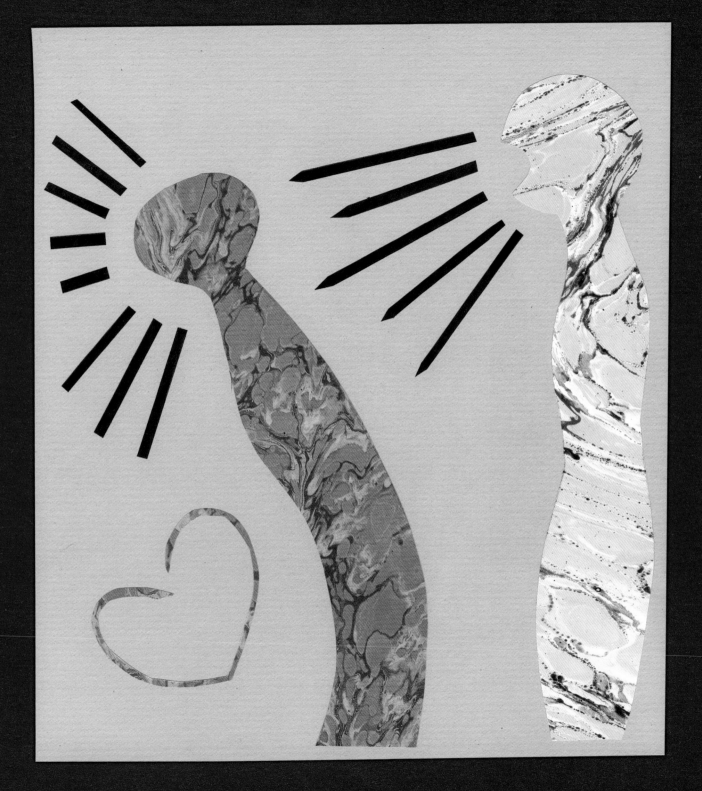

When I was seventeen, a boy drove me to the prom. On the way home, he hit a tree. I hit the windshield. A stranger called my parents. My father drove us to the hospital while my mother stroked my hair. I loved her tender, gentle touch, but I never said a word.

Finally. College. I was happy to go away. My mother and I gave each other stiff hugs goodbye at my dorm room door. I thought I saw tears in her eyes.

I loved living on my own. I seldom thought about my mother. I thought about myself a lot. One summer my mother and I took a trip to see my aunt and we barely spoke. My mother and aunt were still talking about MawMaw.

I graduated from college and went
to London to work in a big office.
When I walked with my briefcase across the
River Thames, I felt like a grown-up. At night
I lay in bed, listening to the lorry's engine and
the train's whistle and Big Ben's bell.

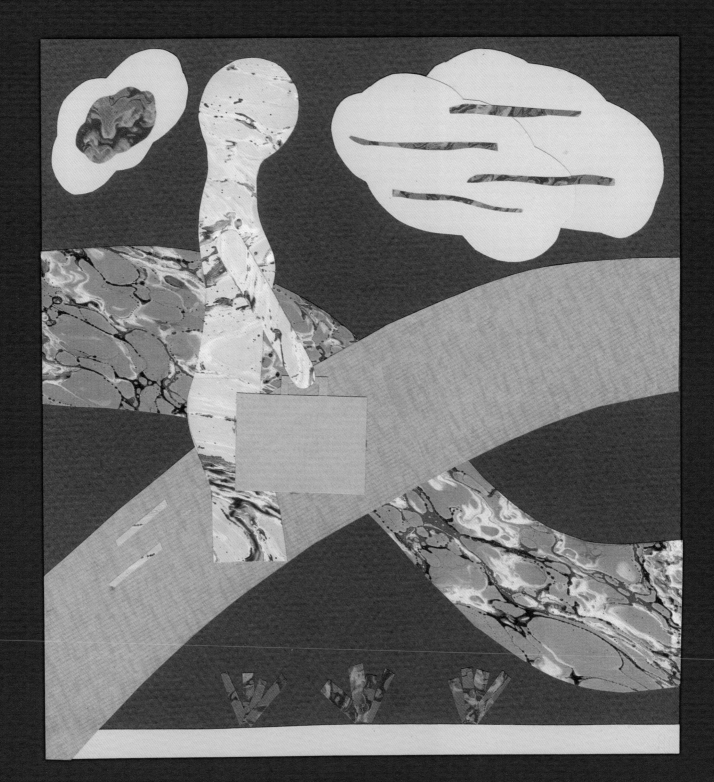

Every week my mother
  wrote a letter to me. She always
  signed it

                    I love you
                    Your Mother

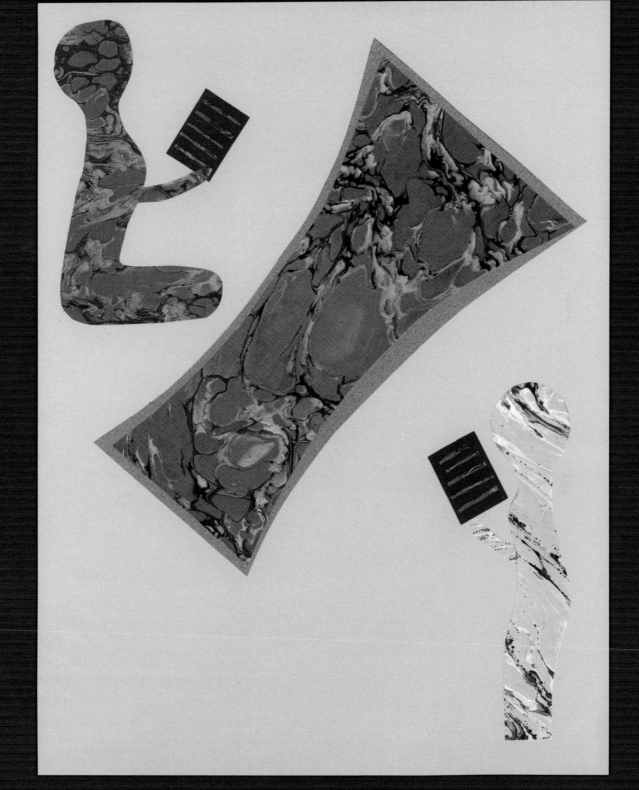

The next year I went to Africa to teach school. I felt grown-up standing by the chalkboard while the students listened. At night I lay on my cot and listened to the villagers chanting and crickets chirping and rain pounding.

Every week my mother wrote a letter to me. She always signed it

I love you
Your Mother

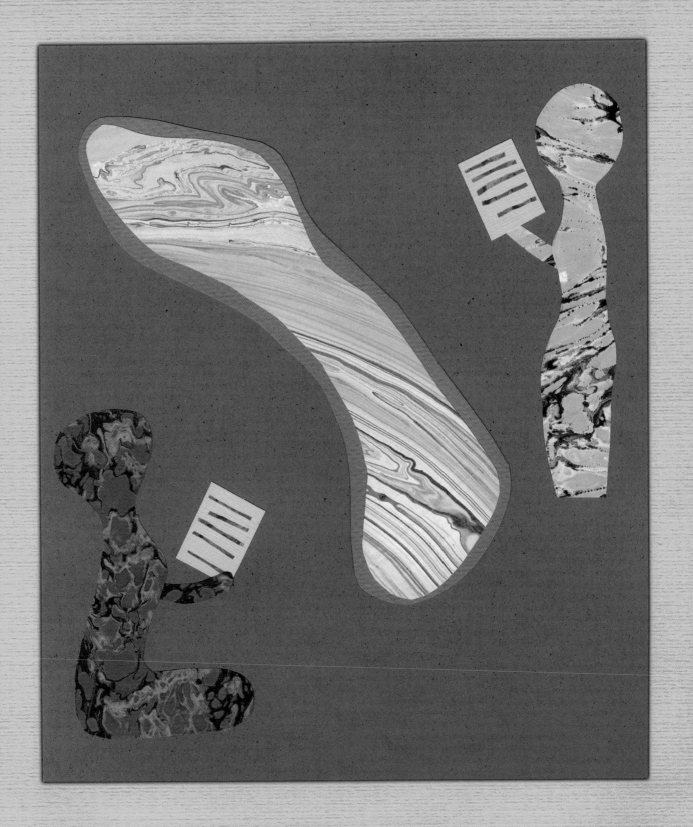

One day a cassette tape came in the mail from my friends and family. Their messages were silly, loud, and loving. My mother sounded formal. "I feel strange talking into a tape recorder," she said stiffly. "So I went to the attic to find your favorite bedtime story." She read each page and her voice was warm and soft. At night I lay on my cot listening to the story again and again.

When I finally came home, the space
between my mother and me had
grown smaller. We talked. We laughed.
One night we went out to dinner with
MawMaw and talked about our dreams.

Through my travels I had met
a tall, sturdy, funny, smart man.
We fell in love and were married.

My husband and I went to movies,
gave dinner parties, and ate at ethnic
restaurants. We made a baby. I was amazed.
"I am pregnant," I told my mother.
"I am too young to be called
'Grandmother,'" she said.

My baby girl was born from my womb and into my arms. I looked over her tender newborn face and felt my heart would break. "I'll always hold you close," I whispered in her ear.

My mother came to greet my daughter. She stayed for a week to fluff the pillows. She brewed the coffee, made the beds, folded the laundry. She held my baby close. You can call me "Grandmother" if you want," she said.

When my daughter climbed down from my arms, she chased balloons across the yard. When she skinned her knee, she wanted me to kiss it. She was strong-willed, independent, delicate, and soft.

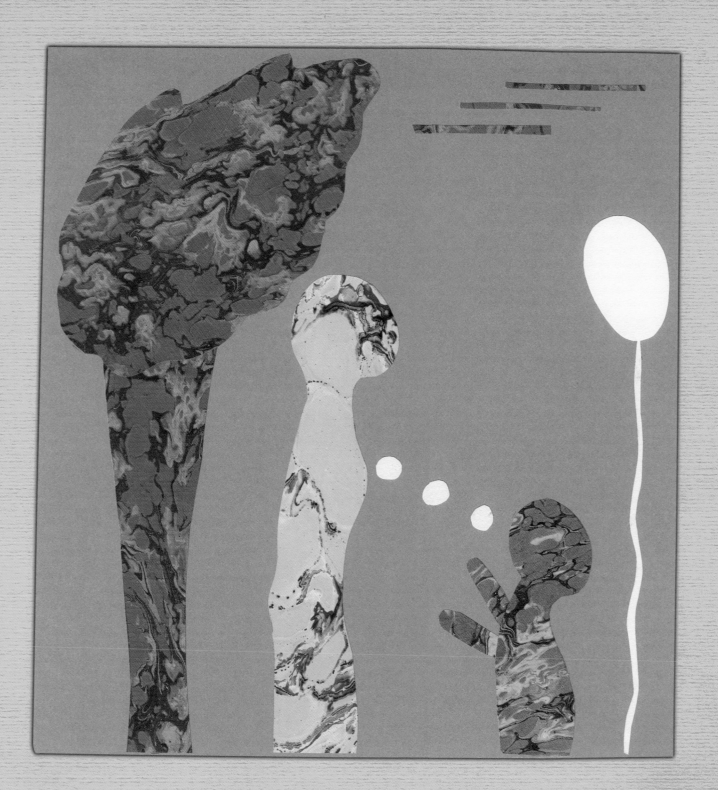

My daughter loved to dance in the living room with her friends. One day I joined them. "Mom, could you please leave us alone?" she asked. "We like to dance by ourselves."

My husband and I took our daughter to the park. We walked through the zoo. We ate peanut butter and jelly.

We made another baby.

My baby boy was born from my womb and into my arms. I looked at his wrinkled perfect face and felt my heart would break. "I'll always hold you close," I whispered in his ear.

My mother came to greet my son. "It's great to be a grandmother," she said. "Grandmothers get to fix ice cream for breakfast, put extra bubbles in the bath and read more than one story at bedtime."

She fluffed the pillows, brewed the coffee, made the beds, folded the laundry.

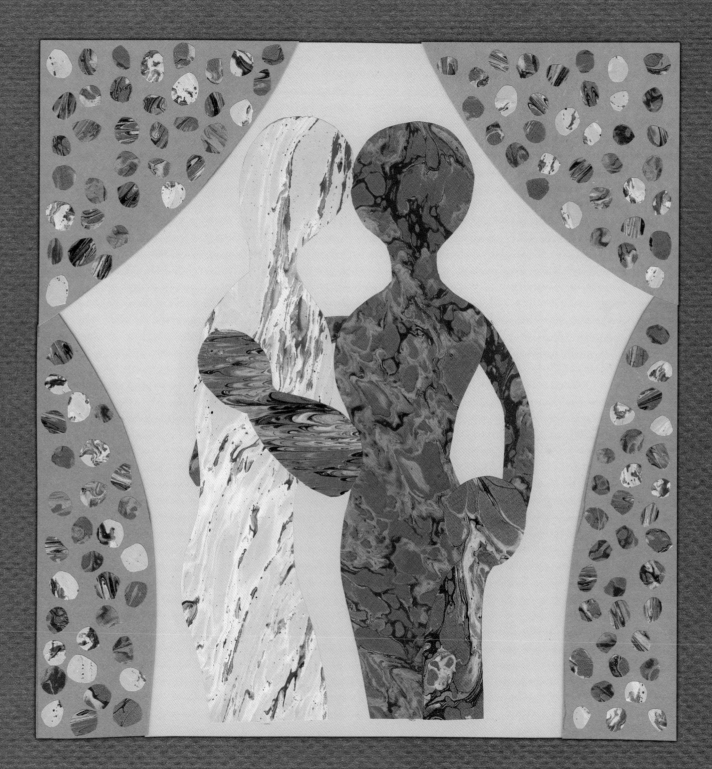

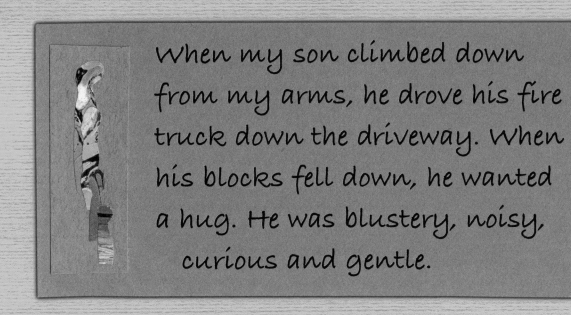

When my son climbed down from my arms, he drove his fire truck down the driveway. When his blocks fell down, he wanted a hug. He was blustery, noisy, curious and gentle.

Now I am the mother who makes the meals, plays the music, drives the carpools. I am also the one who gets tense, angry, and distracted. Sometimes I reach back with a kiss and a hug. Sometimes I don't.

One night my daughter had a piano recital. Her father was running late at the office. I'd spent my day in the car. No one ate the dinner I made. I brushed my daughter's hair too roughly. "Why are you wearing such a grouchy face on my special night?" she asked.

The next morning I called my mother. "Last night I was angry and tense. I said harsh words to your granddaughter. I was grouchy at the recital. I didn't read to her at bedtime. And sometimes she doesn't even want to dance with me."

My mother's voice was gentle. "This is only the beginning," she said. "You both have years of pushing and pulling ahead. Like MawMaw and me. Like you and me. It is the same for you and your daughter. It never ends."

It never ends. I look ahead and wonder what story will unfold with my children. I look back and remember my mother and me, brimming with tenderness and touch, tension and strain.

For now, my children still yell, "Watch me jump, mom!" Most nights I read them bedtime stories. When it's cold, I pile blankets on their beds. Every so often I put parsley on the plate.

I think of my mother every day. Even when she is not near, I see her face, hear her voice, feel her hands. She is still playing, piling, fluffing, brewing, bringing. Each gesture tells me what I've come to know so well:

I love you
Your Mother

The Mother Daughter Dance